Perishable

Perishable

Poems

Stelios Mormoris

Tupelo Press
North Adams, Massachusetts

Perishable
Copyright © 2025 Stelios Mormoris. All rights reserved.
LCCN: 2022921275

Library of Congress Cataloging-in-Publication data is available upon request.

Paperback ISBN: 978-1-961209-19-0
E-Book ISBN: 978-1-961209-24-4

Cover and text designed by Allison O'Keefe
Cover art: Photo by ammar sabaa on Unsplash
Photo by Gayatri Malhotra on Unsplash
Photo by Bruno Martins on Unsplash
Photo by Christoph Gey on Unsplash
Photo by Raul Angel on Unsplash
Photo by Jack B on Unsplash

First edition: April 2025

Other than brief excerpts for reviews and commentaries, no part of this book may be reproduced by any means without permission of the publisher. Please address requests for reprint permission or for course-adoption discounts to:

Tupelo Press
P.O. Box 1767
North Adams, Massachusetts 01247
(413) 664-9611 / Fax: (413) 664-9711
editor@tupelopress.org / www.tupelopress.org

Tupelo Press is an award-winning independent literary press that publishes fine fiction, non-fiction, and poetry in books that are a joy to hold as well as read. Tupelo Press is a registered 501(c)(3) non-profit organization, and we rely on public support to carry out our mission of publishing extraordinary work that may be outside the realm of the large commercial publishers. Financial donations are welcome and are tax deductible.

For Robert Lawrence Cornell

"My heart was wrapped up in clover,
the night I looked at you"
—Etta James

Contents

i. Lamentations

Belle-Île	3
Old Girl	4
Mushrooms	6
The Stream	8
Crossing	9
Indigo	11
Eau de Parfum	12
The Mourner	14
Interruptus	16
Vespers	17

ii. Flora Mortis

Yià Yià	25
In the Roses	26
Baltimore Spring	28
Watermelon	30
Ballerina	32
La Tour Eiffel	35
Homage to Weeds	36
Spangled	38
Arrangements	40
Sigh:	42

iii. Perishable

It Is My Revolution	45
Party at the Mercer	48
Ken & Barbie	50
Jingle-Jangle	52
Ode to Herringbone	53
The Quarrel	54
Perishable	56
Acknowledgments	59

i. Lamentations

Belle-Île

Thistle shoots collected in strata
of violet cliffs, layered

like broken plates of mica.
The sky flattened on the sea offered

its cold lesson of distance.
We waded in the tides' resistance

then dove, the concaves
of our backs spooning the soft waves.

We clasped and took our vows
in the ink-dark undertow

pulling us in unison, our eyes slit
by the horizon

where flirted out of sight
the terrible birds of our derision.

Old Girl

Modesty is the girl
with a smidge of dirt on one cheek
turning down an alley
where the trucks park at lunch.

She smokes out of the side of her mouth
to keep her lipstick
the color of chili, fresh.

Hike them up, old girl,
your soiled pink velour pantaloons
with lime-green drawstrings.

Bend down to tie the little bowties, yes,
and check if you are dead.

Tighten them
then rise and stand
on your scorched satin slippers.

Listen to the chorus of drippings
from the last blue rain
in the copper gutters, and watery grates.

Walk toward me
as the rose-tinged clouds retreat
from this theatre of bohèmes
going all night
like a set of smashed glasses.

Walk toward me, old girl,
pick it up, find your old mean cat
preparing to swirl
and confuse and brighten
the men scotched to their steins.

Unfurl a dance to rills of liqueur
on mirrors of pavestones.
Run your runway, your *fin-de-siècle* ballroom
littered with stars.

Come forward, unloved,
slurring rhinestones and vowels
under your mother's refrains of *mon enfant,*

mon enfant.

Mushrooms

I thumbed the velour gills
of its underside flecked to a lighter gray,
leaving a smudge finer than dust,
ghastly as ashes

settling in my fingerprint
and fluorescent arcs of my cuticles.
The mushroom affixed
its skin to mine.

I grew shadowless
under the canopy of trees,
whittling wind
into a fabric of whispers

until anonymous,
blameless,
I forged the urge
to learn this stranger.

Against my lid I pressed
the iridescent crown,
bruising as I slid
it down the crest of my nose

to inhale its damp, cumulative odor.
The knotted roots
they bred on
led me within earshot

of blackish rushing rivulets
where the sun slipped
furtive knives, and pebbles quarreled
under rhymes of water.

Quiet, not silent,
the mushrooms kept witness.
And in my wake glowed
a silent choir.

The Stream

Elliptic slips of rainbow
along a braid in the stream
follow the skittering arrows
of fleets of salmon who climb
the air at boulders, navigate
films of oak leaf sinking—
striate the currents they migrate
undeterred by limbs collapsing.
Deserted, I find calm in the oar
that lies exiled on the shore,
watching wakes of salmon
whir the water into clear liqueur
and magnify the mossy bottom,
kindling emeralds in sun.

Crossing

breathless
   in the bight's
current, the
   sailor glides
inches above
   horizon's edge
gleaming
   like a knife.

A coral-tinted
   sunset seethes
in ribs of sea,
   blackish where
the sails drag
   ragged shadows
from which he
   can't tear free.

He clenches
   the bristled rope,
rides ebbs of
   pain, those violet
veils of storm
   when he learns
he cannot
   cry or measure.

He tacks away
   from the little
shingled houses
   dotting leeward
shore, watching
   what he loved once
dwindle—skirts
   the last strips

of sun slashing
   the whitecaps'
whispers, races
   along the pin
pricks of light
   on the shore road
into next day,
   into the balm

of sun, sleep.

Indigo

Cobalt light on driven rivers,
flute notes floating in veils of wind
down whistled-out canyons
that issue into fields of tiny bluets
limning the dawn.

A child's face faces the world
like light borne in water blinking awake.
What theatre of stars doesn't expire?
I stand in the night heat
of high summer, unable to gather nettings

of stars imparted with still explosions,
only learning to lose them.
Once I could locate
the tendrils of constellations, always
rearranging like the footprints of a dance

behind whispers of a thousand roofs.
Now they rise out of the fringe of trees,
and drape garlands in the pond
around a wading moon
whose sheath I float mindless through

the city's smoke-laced conversations
caught in the fretwork
of iron balconies.
I sink in blackish water,
and the indigo shroud of the universe lifts.

Eau de Parfum

In the mirror of
winter I long for
sun on the neck,
its scarf of sorrow—
the wild jasmine
and arid cliffs

warm as bread
veiling my face.
I slow the swirling
of the velouté
and turn the spoon
like an oar to blend

the thyme, cream,
and crystals of salt.
I submerge a cloud
and her last perfume,
l'heure bleue, mixed
with hillside laurel

rises over the rim.
Two softened reeds
of rosemary pair
and spin—compass
searching memory.
Ladling dusk, I see

casted nets tagged
with strips of algae
dripping sunlight—
repertoires of scent
fleeing, returning
like ragged kites:

roses and bourbon,
burnt toast, mother's
laundry on the line—
blossoms of gasoline
from her idling car
waning into sunrise.

The Mourner

Was it lover, or brother,
or impossible friend

who lies here
under the gray stone?

A single tear reflects
a sliding moon

absorbed by her black veil.
She turns

into the circular current
of the bay abutting

to smother a cry,
floating away

through a dripping comb
of willow trees.

Blackbirds on the pier
consider flight,

rustling layers
while she freezes

like alabaster
in the echo of a vestibule,

circled by cameos
and heirloom stares.

Fissures down
the disfigured faces

of stoic mothers
and grandmothers

belie the love
underneath the cool

porcelain, aquiline
noses, and cast

lacework and hair.
Bells climb.

She slaps her face,
then steps down

into the canal
of mourners teeming

with private litanies.
Brittle leaves

of pin oaks
detach like dismayed

hands, land
on her hair and cling.

Interruptus

I rescinded
God, latched
shut the red
door, again.
Dried wreath
of eucalyptus
shook; I took
my last wits
squirreled in
my hand like
a fine chain.
I considered
death: lunar
side of crisp
silver knife—
vast wishes
sliced aloft—
like a fleet
of tiny birds,
honing air's
great breath,
while below
dogs barked
at my rising,
and the pond's
eye glittered
blue as snow.

Vespers

i.

I slipped inside you while
you slept. We were halves
of one lung, breathing
in unison, and an altar boy

shepherded a candle
along the winded corridors
of our cage of ribs
joined by cords of sweat.

He marched the clock
of bells into the horror
of the flesh, his erection
compressed under crisp

ironed pants, repeating
the steps from the choir
to the altar and back,
passing the flame faster

between us, this distance
narrowing into a fissured
seam as we grew to love.
Eventually the flame

grew calmer, immutable,
our common ruler, proud
dancer switching on itself,
waxing in its own light.

ii.

I craved being apart
but not alone: to be the
withering light of blue glass
from the transept window

draped over a polished
walnut pew, where you sat
handsome with a tie on,
an animal with folded paws,

hunger and penitence
swaddled in wool and silk.
Under a thunderous sermon
on baptism, I felt the edge

of your thin smile, caught
your thick legs open.
I lapsed into the staccato
of my mother harping

I wear brand new shoes
to church, black cordovan,
too shiny, tight as sin—
that I sip the syrupy wine,

kiss his hand, swallow the
wafer. And then the release:
across you hot wet seed
turning cold and dry.

iii.

Confusion was a basin
of milk, floating strands
of white beads and silver
cross like a fish's fin,

appearing, disappearing.
I clung to raveled limbs
in shadows of plankton
under the aqua lagoon

mirror, flotilla of wishes
in tow: holding hands on
our drive to work, bathing
in a glass bell inverted

in the sea, reciting Kant.
The uncorked wine turns
the Easter lilies brown,
and years sit in estuaries.

I march toward the altar
through the echoes of
sermons—pause, feel the
fingers of your vespers—

graze of your thumb on
my knee's mantle, silent
praise after sex, shadows'
wings riding my shoulder.

ii. Flora Mortis

Yià Yià

The fireflies I caught at four
glowed in a mason jar
of mottled glass.

I left them at the door
of my Yià Yià—
lacquering her hair with hairspray—

—gift from the blonde son
of her dark son,
starved for a cookie or powdered kiss

or coin ridged with pain,
imprinted with the laurel wreath
of a curly-haired king.

When she emerged
all coiffed *à la francaise*,
I touched his face in my pocket,

summoning the trace
of the father I never saw.
I sank and rose in anger's seesaw,

back into her clutch
of faceted rings
and fragrant tendrils of arid rose.

We drove to the beach,
swam inside the swirls of fish
silver as her bracelets,

then glistened like olives.
On the rutted road home, I fell
asleep in the sun on my skin.

After siesta, she poured tea
without trembling
on the shady marble veranda,

in mandarin blossoms.
She half-smiled,
grateful, her cluster of knuckles,

rubies and pearls
tugging the night table
varnished like a vintage violin.

Here in her keep
she kept the fireflies to sleep.
I watched them simmer

a neon green
in the jar's glazed basin
while she whispered to my father:

one curse brings a spring of blessings.
She crossed her heart
with three closed fingers—

the father, the son, the Holy Spirit,
then pressed her palm
to the icon,

its almond eyes eking resinous tears
bathed in red votive.
I set the fireflies

free, lazily rising
out of the glass orifice,
while he lurked in the halo

of a candle
on this dry, flammable night
I couldn't blow out.

In the Roses

I swipe daughter up the feed of my phone

press my nose to a bouquet of buds—
descend inward beyond the roses' symmetry
                        of cluttered folds
with the angst of a girl
hanging on clouds edging closer—

                        remembering how I
blushed my lips on walks to the beach
with rouge-hued rose hips, crushed,
and read thickets of diary,
                        that this was sex.

The scent of rose tattoos
as I plunge through the petals' cool skins,
learning there is no bottom,
                        only descent,
only numbness of speed.

It is, in fact, a form of rising,
and I discern rosettes of smoke, far down,
and a wafer moon
                        which signals winter.

Charred specs of sun fray into focus,
coalesce like flies around a wood-crate pulpit
where my daughter practices her mantra—
mommy, knife, twine, tourniquet—
                        brushing pollen
from her auburn hair,
circled by activists spitting thorns.

                         She recoils
under our phantom arguments,
embers searing on and off—*fuck it, hush*
—into untethered ash.
                         I settle in the reprieve
of the stutter of her fleeing on plazas of stone,
lifting fleets of pummeled petals
which fail to recompose
the buds they exploded from.

Muted between sheets I hang out to dry,
I long for pink roses
pale as a girl's underwear,
                         and dry bouquet
mother left me
on the pilled white bedspread.

And, outside my bedroom,
through the wavering mirage of high summer,

                         the bramble of roses
getting their start on petrified fences.

Baltimore Spring

The streets settle quiet
as embers. A policeman patrols
on a horse past the hollow
mansions of Mount Vernon
and from his saddle slaps a ticket
on a car and moves on.
Far from the centers of crime,
far from his duty,
the stately row of turn-
of-the-century
homes hardly consoles
him: life was civilized one time
and criminals can't learn.

...

Yet the city opens its arms!
On a glorious day
pedestrians lose their way
in a new neighborhood
of brick townhomes and thick trees.
Students of Mahler and Brahms
hum and compose
in the park—on the grass instead
of the benches—while the sweet alarm
of children playing play
like notes against the repartée
of hammers turning houses into homes.

...

Across the cityscape
of a stolen day downtown
sheets of sun drape
two facing towers' sheer glass sides.
And in the chasm between,
the contrasting industrial brick
shows through, reminds
me it is an old city.
Lost in the cross
reflections of strains of glass,
on the brick I find the faded signs
of Home Mutual Life and Scarlett Seeds
under the sound of noon-time traffic,
dangling in another century.

Watermelon

How easily you excavate the outsized
placenta, encased in jungle-green stripes—
cut a smile through its fibrous belly

with sly delight, and serve heaps
of dripping cubed and trapezoidal pieces.
And how greedily the guests partake,

the usual restraint suspended, like a crowd
that springs up to dance, swinging limbs
and hips to express some ravenous,

and embarrassing fetish. Sinking down
through small aqueous explosions,
no one takes a breath while they eat,

as no one observes the hue of the flesh,
dark pink, amenable, almost bawdy—
the id forgotten in luxuriant dissolve.

Only a gourmand would breathe the rind,
thick, wet—cool as a bouquet of wind,
cucumber's sweeter cousin, or consider

swallowing, that is, the slippery seeds
shiny as polished teak. Generous, you
serve babies from the garden, sliced,

which glow against the wooden table—
elliptic halves exposed, poised to perish
under summer sun. A collective thirst

kindles. The merry guests approach
like horses to a spring, amidst tendrils
of barbecue and mustard—slowly at first

with the charade of decorum, drawn by
the promise of water's glinting eyes,
then cast their plastic forks and knives,

unable to cherish, or think, and just dig in.

Ballerina

The oval pool of light
you spin in

quivers
on the lacquered stage

like the flesh
you slip the knife from.

You perfect how you fondle
his weir of sutures.

You flee,
perfect the pulse of each plié.

Kill and repeat.
Rehearsals blur the seasons,

until there is no
line between the show

and grin of footlights
and audience's sea.

Heavy blue curtains drop
on whimpers.

You curtsy with grace
to receding applause.

Pas de deux
under hot moons of kliegs:

his gaze grazes you,
you button up,

float footsteps exit right—
cutouts of chalk

for him to follow
in the unpleating shadows

of the black entr'acte
he cries through.

By the coda
it is clear

he only wants the ballerina,
not the ballet.

Cymbals fray
each breaking pirouette

while tiers of chandeliers
glisten like rain,

his boyish smile
oblong in a dangling crystal.

You lord theatrics
past consent—

revive him in a staccato
of slaps, then vault

adieu in scalloped arcs—
scurrilous cape

sweeping the smatter
of long-stem roses flung

at your feet
brushed into the orchestra pit

to the snap of cases closing
and frivolous flute.

La Tour Eiffel

On a l'habitude de telle commotion:
In its penile crown a chalk-skinned diva of
the Opéra Bastille filmed herself singing Carmen

in a pirate broadcast to the nation,
naked, taut on a bed of petals. She orated *Love
Is a Rebellious Bird* to the gendarmes' amused ovation.

The tapered tower rises, aloof to adulation,
its beacon blinking rubies above
the x-rayed city like a heart without emotion.

Beneath its groin the taxis idle one revolution—
stay within their lanes—while chauffeurs harbor love
for passengers blasé, grazed by neon

tubes along the watery quais. Carousel in motion,
lovers circle the *étoile* in cars, cruise the trove
of parks, close in on their attractions,
and flash their headlights of dispassion.

Around me sizzle concentric belts of traffic,
lumière reduced to gas-fed flames in verdigris lanterns
along this empty *allée*, on whose stones I learn
to walk the loneliness that burns

like final cinders in the flash
of smoke as the tower lights extinguish.

Homage to Weeds

I took a pit stop and warm beer from the seat.
Keys clinked flat against the ignition
long after the stutter of dirt-bumps I sped across
chuckling to dumbass radio shows about weight loss

and love loss and orphaned banjos and a widower betwixt
mauve-shadowed girls, and the plumber who fixed
more than pipes and wore a copper handcuff.
Exhaust dispersed like gnats

as I rolled out of the car under the graze of bees
into the shade of someone's well-loved well-bred flower bed,
face in the dirt on the side I leaned to the screen
in confession, lanky weed next to my nose,

leaves serrated like a knife I pulled in a bar—
its totem of buds hard as cloves,
sturdy as a drunk man who could stagger through court
or wave of sunlight across a field of corn.

The weed was paltry—stripped bare of some
previous glamour—still graced with glove-white flowers,
the petals' unfurling fringe soft as the hem
on the check-out girl in fishnets

who mouthed *kill me* at the start of every prayer.
Strike it up to tattered luck,
to the flint-haired minister scolding from the pulpit
that heaven be damned I chased

her toward the interstate through the gallop of lights—
while the deer-eyed boy greasy as a chassis
bragged he punctured his teacher's
tires, who reeked cologne and forgot to pump the tank full

which is why I petered out of gas
at a bend in the road I mistook for my escape
where congregated thistle, chicory, and Queen Anne's lace—
prickly and intricate and full of trickery.

Spangled

Gauze of afternoon blurs the billboards
in Times Square. Under ledges of marquees
and ads selling Coke and kinetic cross-fit
shoes, below the flow of minus & plus,
tourists mill like dust, almost translucent.

Commuters change shoes fast as windows
blink gray to catch unforgiving trains,
and weekend commences. I fall into
a tall and leggy woman, like a red-tipped
matchstick—perhaps an extra in a matinée?—

or call girl as my mother would say?—or
September-issue girl of *Vogue*, 1984?—
crossing Broadway's stripes of shadow
in a bodice of spangles, flashing her vice—
mass of refraction absorbing hurt and light.

I track behind her, askew in tiny mirrors
on the curve of her hip, shifting me like cargo
in a makeshift train as she walks faster,
swabbed by neon in a blur of faces.
Traffic-light halos cast rings over crowds.

The heart jumps in a swipe of glare,
and knife of skyscraper gleaming.
Under turbans of steam, vendors turn in.
I reach Fifth, caught in a grid of screens
checker-boarding comically my shock

how in tinted reflections I followed her
for blocks. I try to shadow her serpent turns
through fleeing swarms with no design.
Yet lose the view of my sidestep dance,
my boy's delight, breathless in her spangle

as she vanishes into a black well of stairs.

Arrangements

i.

I wonder whether my love
will select the proper flowers:

wreaths of yellow roses on
the altar, the walnut coffin
coated in petals, bouquets of
peony for brother and sisters.

Even now, entranced by incense
filling the transept's gilded dome,
I can see mourners in past tense
flow out the pine doors, numb

with grief kindled by the chorus.
Some friends seem oblivious
under their veils to failures of love,
lost in the hypnotic clacking of

soles on the marble, tight-lipped
and tearless, while grief is tripped
when they least expect, and see
my number in their leather diary

in the hive of the café, parked
on our velour banquettes, chatting
about ailments, heirs and piling
bills, and spouses' indiscretions

in between, sweet clinks of teacup
as friends in lockstep we got up
to unslip hands, with resolutions
armed and tender gloves intact.

ii.

Tombs like headboards ping
the sun, peek through melting
snow. An orange crane lowers
its jowl to remove a boulder

from its frozen socket, rolled
slowly past the grid of dead,
flashing quartz and schist
to fossils of leaves, glinting

like my ugly heirloom ring
brooding in a box—amethyst
and silver. Bereft of grace,
thick grafts of sod peel clean

as they prepare the burial place.
Peering down this vault alone
into the silk-dark sediment,
I shudder I made ceremony

of ceremony with mild glee,
constantly toiling arrangements
as one would tune the strings
of a quartet of violins.

So turn up a thunderous canon
on Deutsche Grammophon
and conjure bells of muguet
to lift, lift in the sunlit repartée

of blues and reds across the pews.
But it is I who will not choose.

Sigh:

It is the slice of the scythe
at the end of its arc
fluttering the seagrass.
It is the farmer finished with
his clearing, sitting on a painted stump
exhaling the milky sunset
his wife stares into from the kitchen
wanting him to love.
It is another bill grinning
with digits—and calendar still curling
from September, 1964.
It is the dead dog
crying in the woods at night,
the ring of a phone
muffled under velvet drapes. It is
the breath of what was.
                                You wait
for morning before sun breaks,
for the omen of breezes
to squirrel up the canal.
On the opposite bank
fields of mustard asters blaze—
all pinwheels and pom-poms and seeds
floating in a haze—
and sigh in one chorus,
thousands of petals grazing each other
like mourners in a congregation
as the casket passes.

iii. Perishable

It Is My Revolution

   at a picnic table on the street
carved with initials like a tablet
   of hieroglyphics, stained with
rings of coffee mugs and glasses
   of craft beer from breweries
steaming in the hill towns behind
   the Sierra Madre, when I scan
my hand across all the couples who
   met here and carved and parted,
and some who fucked and died in
   each other's arms, or someone else's,
or faded in shadowless hospitals,
   generations streaming to the Castro
under the giant nylon rainbow
   that imbued their skins with a light
of a new mother's eyes, brimming.

   And I wonder if it is possible to be
reborn with grace, and erase the old
   tablets we carry on our backs
as we migrate here into this cauldron
   of love, into this kaleidoscope of light
submitting to fog and pellucid pills,
   my back imprinted with the perfect
penmanship of teachers, and crosses
   of mothers and inscriptions of fathers
and swift signatures of lawyers,
   abrupt and dangerous as the knife-tips
of judgment under the sanctity of
   normal, not normal, this cumulative
alphabet scrawled on my back, under
   the leather backpack I finally slip off
on a Greyhound bus with my friend.

    His hand trembles when he offers
his ticket to the driver: destination
    San Francisco—date, fare in typewriter
typeface on this modest cardboard
    passport, imprinting itself forever on
our backs' mindful heavy tablets,
    that this is official, that we are here,
in our Oz, as we step down
    into this etherized world that soon
would be ours: riddled by the buzz
    of streetcars sliding under wires,
and rodeo of radios' wrangling guitars,
    and distant grist of mariachi bands
while drag queens stride down Market
    Street with streamers of melon and lime
attached to their arms like fluttery fins.

    Like ferocious fish armed with teeth
offset by scarlet lips, they lead the charge
    as we finally dig into our heaps
of lumpy guacamole and saffron rice
    in nicked wooden bowls and notice
sitting next to us, side by side, two men
    who slowly embrace and kiss
like interlacing serpents, apparently
    for our benefit, and someone whistles
from a moving car, then the car reverses
    and a tribe of them get out, circle us,
laughing, speaking rapid-fire Spanish,
    and fling   *faggot, pussies, mierda*
while my friend pans his palm over
    our freshly carved initials in the wood,
and we feel the coolness of shadow

of the glorious flag wanting to sink.
One man darts from the well of a
   crowded bar, arms brocaded in tattoos
of multiple alphabets, his *tabula rasa*,
   screams your *faggot is here*, grabs
the tabasco and flicks at the boys
   the hot vial of liquid, breaking the yoke
around us—then slips from his sleeve
   a baton and cracks them, one by one,
swiftly as insults in any language,
   until they crumple on the table, on
our tablets: blood flows like the quiet
   lyric of how deltas swell and form,
and fills the letters while I listen
   to sirens down in the Mission, and

I notice how no one does anything at all,
   except watch the men fade, like the sirens—
the door of their turquoise Impala
   still open in traffic, whose impediment
cars eddy around, and all the choirs of
   the city emerge in collective suspension:
the plastic whisper of streamers, drums
   getting closer, babies' laughs in strollers
as two fathers shake hands in front of
   the theatre running *All About Eve*,
while a window blows opera,
   and a cop approaches with his tablet of
questions, and all I could do is watch
   letters disassemble and float into the fog
above Twin Peaks, above sun-sizzled wires
   and the hymn of voices, rising,

while the men keep on kissing.

Party at the Mercer

You exhaled a long skein
            of indigo smoke in the lobby
     of the Hotel Mercer,
which widened down like a bed sheet
         in drugged-out slow motion
toward the purple carpet
           marred by boot treads of hipsters
singing "Industry Babe" by Lil Nas X.

I was bored with your antics,
         singeing hems at every cackle—
unfinished joints flicked
  against quilted silver
         panels of the elevator carrying
the dead load of us,
        high from our bonuses
and jubilee acrylic trainers.

We rose into the glass penthouse
         studded with chunky rhinestones
     arranged like constellations,
as we calculated where we sat, with whom—
      how we crossed our legs to blunt
the horny bourgeois trash,
        reserve the parting of knees
to leather-padded rainmakers:

The He who slipped out
         the cobalt cobra wallet
soft as a pellucid pill,
the She who shared she despises blow
       jobs and adopted a Laotian baby,
pretending to ignore her killer tits
         with patches of disco glitter—
And the tranny who likened her

transition to crossing the Brooklyn Bridge
                against traffic, screaming in three
     octaves, and we honored her on cue
with crackling refrains of
          "you got it going on, bitch"
and you—yes, you—smiling through the shame
          of two botched drug deals,
and failing your exam by one lousy point,

stroked my forearm
              like the arm of the sofa, its velour
     softer, more helpless, to apologize,
and so I listened to the stream
            of chemical blue vapor, reminding
me of the swirl of light from the camera
            in the perch of the movie theater
in your hometown in Ohio,

your mother calling you for dinner,
            your strong legs propelling you home
     to eat after soccer, to run off bouts
of grief, through the storm
            that riddled the gully in the cornfield
that cradled your father dead as stone,
            and I let your bulbous ass flow
into the bar to fetch a pink martini,

wanting with some wild loyalty
            to see you raising a silver bell—
     as you dwindled in the atonal din
of the clink of the stirrer
            and groan of silk vermouth
sinking to the base of the fluted glass,
            stars blitzing off your zinc zipper
as you held back crying.

Ken & Barbie

Why did my doll look embalmed,
the color of vintage Band-Aids?
For my birthday, sister told me
he was anatomically incorrect,
and couldn't fuck without a penis

which is why we had to slip his
rigid body into any crevice available,
when she squatted and asked me to
insert him between her calf and thigh,
so she could spill her gibberish,

like an oracle, she said, and blurted
you're a faggot, then laughed her hyena
but I knew she was jealous, coiled up
like hair she constantly shampooed
with ash blonde dye called *razzmatazz*.

Doll to my doll, I let my limp-long bangs
hide the embers in my sapphire eyes.
Sister never knew I stole her dresses
never worn, still tethered to price tags,
tinged with the scent of Easter lilies

beside Mama's shiny hickory casket.
How I festooned them under razors
of sunrise between the slats of our barn
before anyone woke, ear cocked to
motors warming up in a commotion.

I hid my brooches' constellation:
Tiger's eye, tourmaline, and moonstone.
Their somnambulist glints conjured
feats of flying: I could spell in smoke,
powder blue, with such fanciful cursive

above Grandpa's farm he would cheer
me frozen from his chair, under his name.
In rumples of sleeve, I propped up doll
to watch me collar Grandpa's lapis
chokers, and even Daddy's bowties on

his daughter's State Fair gingham dress.
Doll never said a word, but praised how
nothing matched—exactly when I felt
my heart burr like a tractor tilling soil.
Lying in our manger of accoutrements—

among cubes of hay birds chittered under—
we heard the barreled men at dawn
careen my Daddy's bourbon then crumple
her on fenders in yellow beams of fog light,
parked outside. She cackled into cries.

Sister bragged she lured a cop once
who licked her freckles ticklish, pressed
his plated star to her nipples' tender
aureoles large as rings of flashlights.
Pretty as a showpig, she said he said.

He filled her under stars with seed
but she always came back empty.

Jingle-Jangle

Jingle-jangle rang your bracelets
when you slapped me,
a teacher spurring me on,
warning me not to bleed my want,
not cry like a dog
despite your murderous
tits, and full mouth, and glittery nails
that pattered on the hollow
of my back when I entered you with abandon,
when you came before I did
and the sky turned coral,
blooming like a bird of paradise.
We braided our limbs across the slippery silk,
futile to untangle as we drifted in
an anteroom of perfume
raveling in coils down leeward shores of skin
tensed for the slightest hiss
of a dirty word.
You sprang out of our dormant mesh
decoupling fingers hooked to
fingers, undulating like a serpent,
darting in and out the gold and silver piercings
in a row on the side of your tongue—
the stereo blasting
a fugue of spangled tambourine—
until you flaunted in your fist the roll of cash
that slipped already
through the slit of desire.

Ode to Herringbone

Its diagonals line up, form
    an elegant ziggurat, not quite
ninety degrees but forty-five,

    dash to slash, awry to askew—
as if someone slit the crossties
    right up the middle then shifted

back the rails evenly on each side,
    altering the zipper and becoming
arrows, in alternating directions.

    The herringbone is neatly packed—
a construct of tightness, the bones
    arranged like files of line-sharp fins.

How cunning to have laid to rest
    the fish sideways in these tiny tins,
marooned in their oil

    at opposing angles. Such economy
of space that yielded design
    on shellacked parquets,

or jackets cloaking cloudy days.
    From afar this wooly twill
reads solid but closer inspection

    reveals its broken skeleton:
like the blustery day I met you
    and discerned a pattern beneath

the pattern I squinted to decipher,
    testing my eye- and foresight
as you betrayed your grains and hues.

The Quarrel

Out of nowhere—who
    knew on such an indigo
night, laced with jasmine?
    —the quarrel crept in
like an uninvited guest,
    drunk, poorly dressed—
crashing the crush
    of crystal clinks, lush
conversation, and proper
    small talk—to find theater.
We huddled to sofas,
    like a litter of commas.

A dark quiet lowered.
    Clouds of tears piled
on the roof, unshed.
    His first words slipped—
whore, bitch, crazyland—
    bouncing like mercury
on the glossy parquet.
    To kindle the repartée,
to love and be whipped
    with a curated glossary
was the game at hand
    we didn't understand.

Until she replied: staccato
    of vertiginous heels—
—rat-a-tat-tat—and squeals,
    as she ran into the kitchen
to break some porcelain.
    We were now in the know,
stuck, fenced in the ring
    with the boxers, exercising.

He turned up the stereo,
    (Miles Davis, I think), and lit
another nasty cigarette.
    Everyone wanted to go.

He vanished to console
    her, wading in a shoal.
But we heard otherwise:
    soft talk, faucet, cries.
The figurative arrows
    flew in a barrage of color,
scarlet tips on slender
    green shafts. The blows:
Who was she? And why?
    The years of unpaid tax.
We recused, on the sly,
    feathers on our backs.

Perishable

As my grandfather and I hugged the shore road in Oyster Bay, New York—
I was six and he was eighty-six—on June 15, 1963, in fact, at 8:23 a.m.
according to his gold Elgin watch—as I turned his freckled wrist toward me
while eating grape ice cubes, and he drew in a dirty wish from his pipe

stuffed with rich earth, moistened with tears as he always seemed to be
fretful about something—that *yià yià* couldn't mount the stairs, or too much
smoke billowed from the exhaust of his green truck, or that the English
lavender lining the pebbled driveway of his client, Mr. Scherrer, parched

after a drought—it was then it struck me how his eyes dark as the blue Aegean
he left for a life in America burdened him, that he could peer into the souls
of flowers—and so he waved to orange daylilies along the shoulders of the road,
welcoming us into this land of estates and privilege, of smiles and patronage—

and how these blooms hadn't a care, lived for a day, sang their hearts out
then molted into oblivion to flags flapping in the harbor—and that he could even
discern in the cracks of paint on a wooden fence, the tired limb of a broken heart—
and, boy, how he read the cashier in a hairnet at the five & dime with cataracts,

nodding to her, and she knew he knew she had the cancer, nodded back,
agreeing she would fight, gave him change, and touched his veiny palm,
and how when the jittery second hand of the clock in town square hit noon,
she would disappear into the soil underneath the gladioli, slack bladed leaves

folded over and over like a flag at a military burial, the pleating neat,
as all these lives need respect even when they expire, and the gist of this all,
is that my *papou* was all smiles, under his moth-eaten hat, wreathed with feathers,
and he turned on the silver radio in his old Ford and egged me to sing along

to Patsy Cline, but I turned the dial to a bunch of dark ladies with coral lipstick
harmonizing at the top of their lungs like the red poppies and pink peonies
in the manicured fields we passed, nothing out of order, even the sunlight
descending like harp strings through the plane trees framing the gilded gates

until we fell upon a bramble of knotty branches cluttered with pear blossom
pale as the inside of my mother's limp forearm I pressed every morning
for her pulse, with Greek coffee, praying she'd wake, and she always did,
triggering the orchards to populate with color, when my grandfather let go

of the brakes, and we glided down a hill into this cauldron of sweet scents
and fresh-cut grass, laughing, and then he touched my long messy blonde hair
radiating sun, to protect him from what the woman had, who infected him,
even with her dark smile, and yes, I was afraid, I admit it, and lifted my hand

to hold his palm in place on the crown of my head, making sure he kept it
there as long as a cluster of robins pecked the grass, and a white hawk
crossed the sky to eye a trident of minnows lurking on the bay's surface
until we pulled into the driveway of the estate, past the stone gargoyles

greening with moss, and ivy so old its leaves were blanched, and grandfather
took my hand to cut laurel, bundle them with twine, and guided me to look deep
inside the cavern of an iris, and take refuge in its voluptuous violet contours
with his hand on my back, as I made my first form of love, his work done,

his knife slipping into its leather sleeve, after which I cut my first bouquet
for the missus, left it in a milk bottle, when she creaked the back door,
weeping too, waving us to come in for iced tea, and we sat at her linoleum table
under which he pinky-hooked my finger while he calmed her with talk

about the seagrass submitting to the rising seas, and tipped his hat
and signaled we must get on, and as soon as we pulled out of the driveway
to the coarse hum of tires crushing soft pebbles, she started to fade into the lawn
to shadows' violins with no solemn witnesses in suits, waving good-bye,

but nothing after this harlequin morning could match the frailty
of his cloudy eyes slit by the glare of his pocketknife pinning me
to the muddy hood, filling me with a rain of tiny silver birds,
dark squall hovering over a harbor of masts stalled in their voyages,

my arsenal of tears building like saline in a mesh, ready to powder
as he slipped the paper ring off his Cuban cigar before his last smoke
and coasted down the serpentine incline under a pelt of rain,
his fist on the gear, his grandiloquent iris turning in on itself.

Acknowledgments

Grateful acknowledgment is made to the editors of the following publications where these poems or versions of them first appeared:

Beyond Words Literary Review: "Perishable"
Café Review: "The Mourner"
Eunoia Review: "Crossing"
FIRE: "Baltimore Spring"
Full Bleed: "Mushrooms"
High Shelf Press: "Belle-Île"
Humana Obscura: "The Stream"
Narrative: "Eau de Parfum"
The Raven's Perch: "Old Girl," "Watermelon"
Sugar House Review: "Homage to Weeds," "Interruptus"
The Lyric: "The Quarrel"
Tupelo Quarterly: "Indigo," "Sigh:"

Many mentors, friends, places, and family have inspired many of the poems, and I dedicate them here:

"Belle-Île" is dedicated to Bruno Maurice.

"Old Girl" tells the story of a homeless prostitute who lived in and around La Place Saint-Sulpice in the 6eme arrondissement of Paris, in the 1990s.

"Crossing" is inspired by the beautiful waters around my home island of Martha's Vineyard, Massachusetts.

"Eau de Parfum" is dedicated to my mother, Margarita Zitis Mormoris.

"Interruptus" is dedicated to those who suffer from chronic mental illness and thoughts of suicide.

"In the Roses" is dedicated to the love between, and struggles of, all mothers and daughters.

I lived at 529 North Charles Street, in Baltimore, MD, on Mount Vernon Park, which inspired "Baltimore Spring," one of my first published poems from 1984.

"Yìa Yìa" is dedicated to my grandmother, Catherine Mitsopoulos Mormoris.

The writing of "Ballerina" is an amalgam of all the beautiful ballerinas maligned in their real lives and in characters I have seen them perform at the New York City Ballet, Opera Garnier in Paris, Boston Ballet, and Epidaurus over the last twenty years.

The writing of "Homage to Weeds" was inspired by a trip to the beautiful town of Harpers Ferry, West Virginia, in May 1984.

"Party at the Mercer" is dedicated to David Hunter Hathaway.

"It Is My Revolution" honors the first generation of LGBQT+ activists from the 1960s and 1970s who paved the way for the relative equality we as a society enjoy in the US today.

"Ken & Barbie" is dedicated to Mattel, Inc., who invented seemingly innocent dolls (Barbie debuted in 1959, and Ken in 1961) that unwittingly challenged notions of gender and sexuality for generations of American children and adults.

"The Quarrel" is an homage to one of my favorite poets, Howard Moss.

The title poem, "Perishable," is dedicated to my grandfather, George Zitis, an immigrant florist, whose memory as a loving, simple, and strong grandfather stays with me. This poem captures the halcyon days we spent together fishing and gardening, in and around Oyster Bay, New York.

About the Author

Stelios Mormoris is a resident of Boston and Martha's Vineyard, Massachusetts, and formerly lived in Paris most of his life, working as an executive in the beauty industry. Stelios is currently Chief Executive Officer of Scent Beauty, Inc. He studied architecture at Princeton University, where he received his BA, and received his MBA from INSEAD (Institut d'Européen d'Administration des Affaires) in Fontainebleau, France. He has held positions on the boards of the French Cultural Center of Boston, ACT-UP, Historic New England, and the Fragrance Foundation.

Stelios' interests range from rugby to sailing to gardening, while continuing his passion for reading and writing poetry. *Perishable* is his second collection of poetry.

Colophon

This book was set in **Essonnes.**

Inspired by the Didot family of typefaces that
originated in late eighteenth- and early nineteenth-
century France,
it was designed and created by
James Hultquist-Todd of JTD (James Todd Design).

For more information see
https://jtdtype.com/typeface/Essonnes/3.